Specimen Aural Tests

Grades 6-8

for Practical exams

The Associated Board of the Royal Schools of Music

General Notes

In the examination, the examiner will be seeking to assess the candidate's aural awareness and will be ready to prompt if necessary where there is hesitation. For any test which requires a 'sung' response, pitch rather than the vocal quality is the object. The examiner will bear in mind the vocal compass of the candidate, who may sing (to 'lah' or any vowel sound) or may whistle or hum.

Aural tests are marked at all grades out of a maximum of 18, with 12 marks required for a pass. An overall mark is awarded on the basis of the accuracy and speed of the response to the tests. The following marking criteria apply:

	All Grades
(18)	Quick and perceptive response
(15–17)	Good response
	Minor errors or hesitation
(12–14)	An adequate response
	Some hesitation and error
Below Pass standard:	Slow response
(11 and under)	Inaccuracy in majority of tests

Candidates with hearing impairment may opt for alternative tests if requested at the time of entry. Candidates who are visually impaired may request enlarged versions of tests 6B, 7B and 8B, at the time of entry.

Keyboard Harmony is no longer available as an alternative to the aural tests. Candidates wishing to develop this area of work should take the appropriate Practical Musicianship examinations.

Test 6A

GRADE 6

To sing or play from memory the *upper* part of a two-part phrase played twice by the examiner. The key-chord and starting note will first be sounded and named, and the pulse indicated. A second attempt will be allowed if necessary.

© Alfred Lengnick & Co. (a division of Complete Music Ltd)
reprinted by permission

© Israeli Music Publications Ltd
reprinted by permission

6A (cont.)

Allegro   Handel

9

mf *staccato*

Moderato   D. Scarlatti

10

p ⎯⎯ *mf*   *p*

[Moderato]   Beethoven

11

p

Andante   Kirchner

12

p

Minuet   Haydn

13

mf

Vivace   Telemann

14

mp ⎯⎯   *mf*   *mp*

Rondo ♩ = 88   Hummel

Allegro   Mozart

Vivace   J.S. Bach

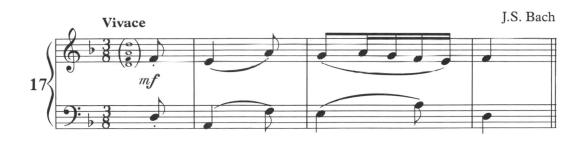

Allegro   D. Scarlatti

Allegro   Rathgeber

Test 6B

To sing a short melody from score, with an accompaniment played by the examiner, in any major or minor key up to three sharps or flats. The key-chord and starting note will first be sounded and the pulse indicated. Candidates may choose to sing the test from the treble or bass clef. A second attempt will be allowed if necessary.

Treble clef

5

6 Schubert

7 English Traditional

8 Cornelius (adapted)

6B (cont.)

Beethoven

Allegro

9

Bass clef

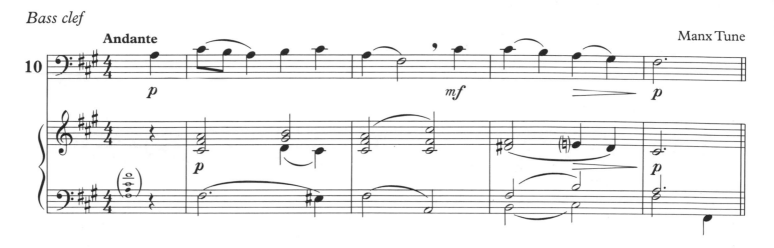

Manx Tune

Andante

10

Hummel (adapted)

Allegro

11

Cornelius (adapted)

Allegretto

12

Test 6C

To identify the cadence at the end of a phrase, played twice by the examiner, as perfect or imperfect, and to state whether it is in a major or minor key. The key-chord will first be sounded.

6C (cont.)

Allegro non troppo

Burgmüller

Molto moderato

Tchaikovsky

Allegretto

Stanford

Tempo di mazurka

Grechaninov

Moderato

English folk tune

Andante

Beethoven

Test 6D

(i) To answer questions on the features of a piece played by the examiner, including the general perception of texture, form (including phrase structure), style and period, of which the examiner will select one or two and advise the candidate accordingly before playing the piece. Candidates will be expected to use Italian terms in their answers where appropriate.

(ii) To clap the rhythm of a short extract played twice by the examiner from the above piece and state whether it is in 2, 3 or 4 time. [The extracts concerned are indicated by ⌐‾‾‾‾‾¬. In the examination they will be played without accompaniment.]

Haydn

(a) About form: *Describe the form of this piece.*
(b) About phrase structure: *What structural feature did you notice in each phrase of the second half?*
(c) About style: *What kind of courtly dance is this?*
(d) About texture: *Describe the texture of this piece.*
(e) About period: *In which period do you think this piece was written? Name a possible composer.*

(a) About phrase structure: *What was the length, in bars, of each phrase?*

(b) About style: *This piece is a dance. What rhythmic feature did you notice? What kind of dance is it?*

(c) About texture: *Describe the texture of this piece.*

(d) About tonality: *Was the piece chiefly major or minor? Where did you notice any difference?*

(e) About period: *In which period do you think this piece was written? Name a possible composer.*

(a) About texture: *What did you notice about the texture of this piece?*
(b) About melody: *Comment on the treatment of the melodic line in the final section.*
(c) About tonality: *Did the tonality change during the piece? In what way?*
(d) About dynamics: *What did you notice about the dynamics?*
(e) About character: *Describe the general character of the piece.*

Semplice, cantabile

Palmgren (adapted)

(a) About structure: *What similarities and differences did you notice between the first and last sections?*

(b) About texture: *Describe the texture of this piece.*

(c) About dynamics: *What did you notice about the dynamics?*

(d) About rhythm: *In the closing section, were the continuous semiquavers in the top, middle or bottom of the writing?*

(e) About style and period: *In which period do you think this piece was written?*

(a) About rhythm: *What rhythmic feature did you notice at the start of most phrases?*
(b) About texture: *In what way did the accompaniment of the middle section differ from the outer sections?*
(c) About tempo: *Did the tempo remain constant? Tell me what happened.*
(d) About dynamics: *Tell me what you noticed about the dynamics in this piece.*
(e) About period: *In which period do you think this piece was written? Name a possible composer.*

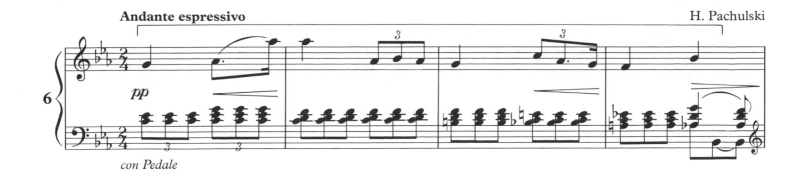

(a) About texture: *Describe the texture of this piece.*
(b) About phrase structure: *In what way were the first two phrases related?*
(c) About tonality: *Was the piece chiefly major or minor? Where did you notice any difference?*
(d) About dynamics: *Describe the dynamics in this piece.*
(e) About style and period: *Comment on the style of this piece. In which period do you think this piece was written?*

Test 7A

To sing or play from memory the *lower* part of a two-part phrase played twice by the examiner. The key-chord and starting note will first be sounded and named, and the pulse indicated. A second attempt will be allowed if necessary.

Allegretto   D. Scarlatti

9

Moderato   Morley

10

Gently   Scottish air

11

Moderato   Burgmüller

12

Allegro   Rossini

13

Andante   Hungarian folksong

14

7A (cont.)

Beethoven (adapted)

Mendelssohn

Robert O. Edwards

Flemish air

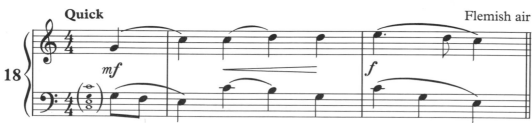

Dunhill

Dunhill (adapted)

Test 7B

To sing a short melody from score, accompanied by a lower part played by the examiner, in any major or minor key up to four sharps or flats. The key-chord and starting note will first be sounded and the pulse indicated. Candidates may choose to sing the test from the treble or bass clef. A second attempt will be allowed if necessary.

Treble clef

7B (cont.)

Bass clef

Test 7C

(i) To identify a cadence at the end of a phrase, played twice by the examiner, as perfect, imperfect or interrupted. The key-chord will first be sounded.

(ii) To identify the two chords forming the above cadence as tonic, subdominant, dominant, dominant seventh or submediant in root position, or tonic in second inversion. Candidates may alternatively use the equivalent roman notation. The key-chord will first be sounded and each chord played again. [The chords to be identified are marked *.]

Andantino Wilm (adapted)

7

Menuet Haydn (adapted)

8

Moderato English Traditional carol melody

9

[Andante] Palestrina (attrib.)

10

Moderato Arne

11

Andante Tchaikovsky

12

Test 7C

(iii) To identify whether a short passage, played once by the examiner, beginning in a major key modulates to its dominant, subdominant, or relative minor. The key-chord will first be sounded and named. Candidates may alternatively state the letter name of the new key.

Test 7D

(i) To answer questions on the features of a piece played by the examiner, including the general perception of texture, form (including phrase structure), style and period, of which the examiner will select one or two and advise the candidate accordingly before playing the piece. Candidates will be expected to use Italian terms in their answers where appropriate.

(ii) To clap the rhythm of a short extract played twice by the examiner from the above piece and state whether it is in 2, 3, 4 or 6/8 time. [The extracts concerned are indicated by ⌐￣￣⌐. In the examination they will be played without accompaniment.]

(a) About texture: *Describe the texture of this piece.*
(b) About form: *What contrapuntal form describes the manner in which each voice or part appears for the first time in this piece?*
(c) About tonality: *Is there any change of tonality in this piece?*
(d) About style: *Tell me about the style of this piece.*
(e) About period: *In which period do you think this piece was written? Why do you think that?*

Frescobaldi

[Allegretto]

(a) About rhythm: *What rhythmic device occurred in the second phrase?*
(b) About structure: *This piece falls into four-bar sections. How many sections are there?*
(c) About texture: *Describe the texture of this piece.*
(d) About tonality: *What did you notice about the tonality of this piece?*
(e) About style and period: *In which period do you think this piece was written? Name a possible composer.*

7D (cont.)

(a) **About form:** *Describe the form of this piece. Did you hear the opening material again? Where?*
(b) **About texture:** *Comment on the texture. Does it remain the same throughout?*
(c) **About dynamics:** *Were the changes of dynamics usually gradual or sudden? When phrases were repeated, was the second time louder or softer?*
(d) **About shape of phrases:** *Did the melody normally move by step or leap? Did it rise or fall at the cadences?*
(e) **About period:** *In which period do you think this piece was written? Name a possible composer.*

(a) About texture: *Was the flowing melody in the top or bottom part? Describe the texture of the accompaniment.*

(b) About dynamics: *Describe the dynamics in this piece.*

(c) About tonality: *Comment on the tonality in this piece.*

(d) About phrase structure: *In what way were the two shorter phrases in the middle of the piece related?*

(e) About style and period: *Comment on the style of this piece. In which period do you think it was written?*

Edward MacDowell

(a) About phrase structure: *The main phrases were four bars long. How long were the phrases added at the end of the two main sections?*
(b) About style: *What features contribute to the style of this piece?*
(c) About texture: *Describe the texture of the accompaniment in the first two phrases.*
(d) About dynamics: *What did you notice about the dynamics? Were the changes always sudden?*
(e) About period: *In which period do you think this piece was written? Why do you think that?*

(a) About texture: *What did you notice about the texture of this piece?*

(b) About rhythmic features: *What rhythmic feature characterised the accompaniment? What did you notice about the rhythm of the second melodic phrase?*

(c) About melody: *Was the melody always in the upper part? Where did it change?*

(d) About tonality: *Describe the tonality of this piece.*

(c) About period: *In which period do you think this piece was written? Name a possible composer.*

Test 8A

GRADE 8

(i) To sing or play from memory the *lowest* part of a short three-part phrase played twice by the examiner. The key-chord and starting note will first be sounded and named, and the pulse indicated. A second attempt will be allowed if necessary. [The lowest part, to be sung or played, is bracketed └─────────┘.]

(ii) To identify the cadence at the end of a further (following) phrase, played twice by the examiner, as perfect, imperfect, interrupted or plagal. The key-chord will first be sounded.

(iii) To identify up to four chords in the above cadential progression, played twice by the examiner, as tonic (root position, first or second inversions), supertonic (root position or first inversion), subdominant (root position), dominant (root position, first or second inversions), dominant seventh (root position), or submediant (root position). Candidates may alternatively use the equivalent roman notation. The key-chord will first be sounded. [The chords to be identified are marked *.]

Test 8B

To sing a short melody from score, accompanied by a higher part played by the examiner, in any major or minor key up to four sharps or flats. The key-chord and starting note will first be sounded and the pulse indicated. Candidates may choose to sing the test from the treble or bass clef. A second attempt will be allowed if necessary.

Treble clef

Bass clef

39

Test 8C

To identify two modulations, each played once by the examiner, beginning in a major or minor key. The passages may modulate to the dominant, subdominant, relative minor or major, or (from a major key only) to the supertonic minor. Candidates will also be required to name the new keys. In each instance the key-chord will first be sounded and the key named.

Test 8D

To discuss matters relating to any of the musical features of a piece played by the examiner.

Note:
The emphasis will be on the candidate providing relevant information in a short discussion on the selected topics, rather than on responses to direct questions. Candidates should be prepared to respond to open-ended invitations, such as 'Please comment on any particular feature you found interesting.' The areas indicated show some aspects on which examiners might prompt a candidate for detail. The first specimen has been annotated to indicate the level of perception expected at this grade. In drawing the discussion to a close, the examiner will normally invite a suggestion as to the style or period in which a piece was written, and (where appropriate) a possible composer.

Candidates may find it beneficial in their preparation to use the specimens set for Test D at Grades 6 and 7, adapting their manner and depth of response to the features listed under each example.

(a) About tonality *(chromaticism)*
(b) About structure and form *(imitation, part-writing)*
(c) About texture *(counterpoint)*
(d) About style and period

In their answers to the above questions, candidates might be expected to notice the shape of the theme/subject (repeated notes followed by a chromatic descent) and that the theme appears in notes of half the value (diminution) in the final section over a repeated bass note (an extended pedal point). Candidates might also notice the highly ornamented cadence typical of the period.

Andantino con tenerezza

Heller (adapted)

(a) About texture *(position of melody, nature of accompaniment)*
(b) About phrase structure
(c) About tonality
(d) About dynamics
(e) About mood and style

Allegro vivace

Beethoven (adapted)

(a) About structure and form
(b) About texture *(thickening of dotted minim motif, texture of **pp** section)*
(c) About phrase-lengths
(d) About dynamics
(e) About style and period *(including appropriate composer)*

Elgar

(a) About structure *(including comparison of the two main sections)*
(b) About tonality *(including comparison of the two main sections)*
(c) About dynamics
(d) About texture
(e) About style and period

(a) About style *(dance form)*
(b) About rhythm *(emphases, cross-rhythm in closing section)*
(c) About tonality
(d) About dynamics
(e) About period

Printed and bound in Great Britain by
Caligraving Limited Thetford Norfolk